Victory to Victory

TRIUMPH THROUGH PAIN

VICTORY TO VICTORY:
Triumph Through Pain

ISBN: 9-798395-141477
Copyright © 2023 by Rebecca Trammell

TABLE OF CONTENTS

ACKNOWLEDGEMENTS

I want to thank my husband David for being my biggest encouragement when I'm writing books. I also want to thank Rev. Anthony and Danielle Miller. Without their expertise in editing and production, this book would not be possible. Finally, my friend Barbara Molter has been my prayer partner and one that I share my thoughts about my book as I'm writing it. Thank you all for what you have done to make this a reality.

FOREWORD

The lyrics to an old song keep rippling through my mind. *"Before every victory, there's a battle to fight and before every sunrise one must live through the night."*

This book was given to my mom throughout a battle. In these devotions you will find words that were written on good days, bad days, and all of the in-between. Instead of folding up and declaring God not to be as good as we all had originally thought, she turned her trial into something that would encourage others in the midst of their own trials. It is beautiful to see God use someone else in the midst of their struggle to grab a hold of someone else and pull them through.

All my life I've known my mother as an encourager, a genuine person whose desire is to touch others and leave them better than she found them.

Through these devotionals I believe your faith will be built and you can began to replace thoughts of worry and defeat with thoughts of faith, hope and victory!

James 1:12 says, "Blessed is the man who perseveres under trial, because when he has stood the test, he will receive the crown of life that God has promised to those that love Him."

Farrah Erwin

LIVING FROM VICTORY TO VICTORY
TRIUMPH THROUGH PAIN

One day as I surveyed the trouble across the world, it started stealing my joy and peace. I cried out to God, *"What am I going to do with all this chaos I see and feel? Life feels very unpredictable."* I then decided to turn the radio to a religious station and have someone speak clarity to my mind.

The preacher spoke out in a message on the radio: "**Live Victory to Victory**". My soul leaped within me. That was it! I need to live from victory to victory. Every day, my God never ceases to amaze me with His promises and answers to my biggest or smallest prayers.

So this book was birthed, *Victory to Victory, Triumph Through Pain*. As I endured some pain and sickness I wasn't expecting, as I navigated each day through pain and discomfort I never wanted to endure, God began to give me words of encouragement that could now help someone else through their troubled times.

So whatever problem you find yourself in today, Praise Him for the victory and you will triumph through the pain in Jesus' name.

SOMETIMES ALLELUIA,
SOMETIMES PRAISE THE LORD

The Lord is good, a stronghold in the day of trouble; and He knows those who trust in Him.
Nahum 1:7

Sometimes trials come out of nowhere. You're trying to live the best you can and do what's right in the sight of God. Yet a trial appears and strikes you. After the blow, you doubt yourself and believe the enemy's lies.

As you cry out in prayer for clarity on the situation, let the Lord know you want to do the best you can for His glory – then fast and pray so God can give you discernment about your situation. God will give you peace to walk this road, even if it's a trial to perfect you or someone else. That's when you ask God to give you a song.

He gave me this: *Sometimes it's Hallelujah, Sometimes it's Praise the Lord*. The main thing to keep in mind is that whatever you're going through, you and Jesus need to stay close through prayer and trust that your trial will only make you better.

Sometimes Alleluia,
Sometimes praise the Lord
Sometimes gently singing,
Our hearts in one accord

Oh let us lift our voices,
Look toward the sky and start to sing
Oh let us now return His love,
Just let our voices ring
Oh let us feel His presence,
Let the sound of praises fill the air
Oh let us sing the song of Jesus' love,
To people everywhere.
Sometimes Alleluia,

Sometimes praise the Lord
Sometimes gently singing,
Our hearts in one accord

Written by Chuck Girard

JUST ANOTHER TOUCH

Our soul waits for the Lord;
He is our help and our shield.
Psalms 33:20

The old song says,
Just another touch, Lord, from You,
To help in hard trials I go through;
Though dark may be the night,
You'll send a ray of light,
When I get a touch, Lord, from You…

I have been going through a season in my life where I experienced ongoing pain in my body. When day after day you experience chronic pain it drains your spirit and your strength. It has caused me to pray more for everyone I hear of that is dealing with pain. It has caused me to reach out to God for strength for the day.

When I wake up each morning, I ask God to "give me a song today". The song came to mind one day, *Just Another Touch Lord*.

I'm so glad we know a God that knows all about us. When you go to doctors and they just shake their head not knowing how to help, He knows what's causing the pain. Just one touch from Him and it will be gone. In the interim period, I'm praising and trusting God. When I awake in the morning facing another day, not knowing what kind of day I will have, I can sing melodies unto the Lord.

Knowing I'm His child, that He loves me and knowing that "just another touch Lord from you," I know I will make it through this day, just fine, with a testimony.

COME HOLY SPIRIT, I NEED THEE

The Lord takes pleasure in those who fear Him, in those who hope in His mercy.
Psalms 147:11

There is no better comfort to have access to — when you are going through a bad time call out to God, "Come, I need You".

Our family and friends want to help us, but as human beings their help can wear out before our trial or sickness is over.

The best comfort to have is between you and God and praying the words to this song. God never grows weary of our needs. He knows our pain, our needs, and when we call out to Him in prayer and worship, He listens. Oh the peace, joy, and comfort that comes to us.

Come, Holy Spirit, I need you
Come, sweet Spirit, I pray
Come in your strength and your power
Come in your own gentle way

Come as a rest to the weary
Come as a balm to the sore
Come, Lord, as strength to my weakness
Fill me with joy evermore

I'M IN IT, BUT I'M COMING OUT OF IT

*And they overcame him by the blood of the
lamb and the word of their testimony, and they
did not love their lives to death.*
Revelation 12:11

I had been sick for several months. Not where I couldn't go anywhere, but I did not feel my best and was not able to do things as usual. I had to have a lot of rest time. I was in bearable pain, but it still drained me and my spirit. My family could see it and I knew it distressed them because I wasn't the same person they knew. I sought out many doctors, and they kept trying to find out my problem, but couldn't. I was becoming downcast, because this affliction was never ending.

One day I got tired of not having anything good to say when people asked me how I was. I remembered hearing a sermon one time and all I recall was the title: "I'm in it but I'm coming out of it".

So from then on when I was asked how I was doing, I'd say "getting better everyday". I'm in it, but I'm coming out if it. God honored my faith, and I started coming out of it. One day at a time I started seeing God's hand at work in my life.

Then, I noticed God was moving in my spirit:

Waking me up to pray in the night.
Touching me during an awesome prayer time.
Prompting me to write devotionals again.

I hadn't felt or been inclined to do these things lately, and I began to praise God for what He was doing in my life. We just never know why we are suffering, and can't make sense of our circumstances, but with God nothing that we go through is wasted. Trials refine us, and make us usable in His kingdom. Together, let us just declare that we are in it, but coming out if it — in Jesus Name!

LEAVING YOUR SO-CALLED
SAFETY FOR HIS CALLING

And every one that hath forsaken houses, or brethren, or sisters, or father, or mother, or wife, or children, or lands, for my name's sake, shall receive an hundredfold, and shall inherit everlasting life.
Matthew 29:19

We had felt called to travel to Europe during the end of the COVID-19 pandemic. I thought the pandemic was ending, but it seemed to be having a resurgence as everything kept pointing to us going to Europe to preach for about six weeks. I started having feelings like:

"What am I doing?"

"I'm older now, other minister's wives at my age don't always go."

"I could stay home close to my daughter, son, and grandkids and play it safe and comfortable."

"Lord I just don't know if I can do this."

"If everything was normal…"

I love traveling overseas, but this is looking like a total walk of faith. Just that quick, as soon as I had those thoughts, Matthew 29:19 came to mind. No one has left houses or lands, mother, father, sisters, or brothers that hasn't been rewarded a hundred fold. God was tuned into my thoughts.

I began to look forward as this trip was ordained of God. No matter what, He will be with you and see you through.

YOU CAN TRUST THE ONE
THAT DIED FOR YOU

"We are troubled on every side,
yet not distressed; we are perplexed,
but not in despair…"
II Corinthians 4:8

As we went to churches raising money for our up coming trip to Europe to evangelize people would ask me, "Are you looking forward to your trip?" I would reply, "If there wasn't a pandemic, I would be very excited!"

I love Europe. We have churches and people we have made friends with, and this could be very exciting and rewarding. But the pandemic kept creeping into my thoughts. What if *this* happens, what if *that* happens. What would I do?

Then God let me read a devotional that touched me right in my innermost being. It was called, *You Can Trust the One That Died For You*. I hear you Lord, it's not by might or by strength it's by Your spirit.

II Corinthians 4:8-10 talks about being troubled on every side but not distressed. Sometimes trouble rolls in like a bad storm. Yet if you know your God, the trouble on every side is getting ready to turn into a victory, to be told every where you go.

God has never forsaken or forgotten his children and He won't start now. We can be so sure in whom we believe. If you never had a problem, how would you know He will never forget you or forsake you? The saying is true: it takes a test to have a testimony. Can you remember the times He has brought you out with a mighty hand?

Ecclesiastes 4:11 tells us, *"He that observeth the wind shall not sow; and he that regardeth the clouds shall not reap."*

Those who wait for certainty before they act may therefore wait forever. Better to sow and reap when you can, trusting God for the results.

The prophet Jeremiah built the wall in troublesome times. What God sent him to do was not popular or well received. But God sent him, and he was called the "weeping prophet" as he fulfilled what he was sent to do.

Daily the enemy is trying to find ways to discourage you. Occasionally you may have a day off, but if you're truly trying to make a difference in this world, the enemy is stalking you trying to get you off course. I had a day when I was pondering yet another troubling situation. I wondered in my mind, *"God, is there* ever a time without a problem?" And just as that thought entered my mind the Lord impressed me with encouragement from his word.

These things I have spoken unto you, that in me ye might have peace. In the world ye shall have tribulation: but be of good cheer; I have overcome the world.
John 16:33

VICTORY IS MINE

Victory is mine, victory is mine,
Victory today is mine.
I told Satan to get thee behind,
Victory today is mine.

I was traveling down the back roads to a neighboring town. I had been bothered by a sickness for two years and it was altering my life. I was tired of it. I had a church family that was praying for me that I would be delivered, yet I felt that this sickness was changing my outlook and dreams for my life, which was traveling with my husband ministering in churches abroad.

I didn't know when the sickness would manifest itself so I was feeling safer at home. As I was traveling that road on a very beautiful Autumn day, the trees were at their color-change peak.

As I was listening to that song, *Victory is Mine*, I felt a victory jolt and hope that leapt within me. I threw up one hand and declared, "I don't have to be sick, I can be healed!" I knew the spot that He touched me.

The miracle didn't fully come at that moment, but the faith He placed in my heart made me know it was on its way. God truly is a miracle worker who never wastes a situation. He worked on me the whole time, knocked off some of my rough edges and willful ways that He couldn't use. He adjusted my thinking to fit His plans. He loosened my grip on the selfish desires I had, and refocused me in His will and ways.

When He speaks victory over your situation, hold onto it with faith. It's coming! Maybe not today or tomorrow, but it's coming.

I AM THE GOD THAT HEALETH THEE

I am the God that healeth thee
I am the Lord your healer
I sent My word and I healed your disease
I am the Lord your healer

I still remember the time and place as I listened to the song *I am the God That Healeth Thee* – when it felt like God Himself spoke to me those words with a booming voice.

I had been battling an illness for so long I was very weary. Oh so weary. Then these words seemed to boom at me out of the heavens. Cleansing, healing tears just flowed out of me for two hours. I went from rejoicing to interceding for lost souls and loved ones.

And said, If thou wilt diligently hearken to the voice of the Lord thy God, and wilt do that which

is right in his sight, and wilt give ear to his commandments, and keep all his statutes, I will put none of these diseases upon thee, which I have brought upon the Egyptians: for I am the Lord that healeth thee.
Exodus 15:26

I wish I could say I wasn't sick another day after that, but I still battled days of sickness. But through it, I could tell I was getting better and I hung onto the promise and the hope that the Lord gave me, that it would come to an end. And it did.

GOD STILL ANSWERS PRAYER

As for me, I will call upon God;
and the Lord shall save me.
Psalms 55:16

I had a long time friend that was devoted to God go through a trial of great magnitude. She lost her beautiful home and continued on without a home for a long period of time. I couldn't understand why she was going through this, and I would daily lift her up in prayer and try to figure out in my mind how I could solve her problems, since God was taking His time.

I would be constantly looking for her a house that maybe I could afford to buy, every time I would find something God would stop me. I remember one service where the preacher said, "We don't know what people are going through that come to church". They may smile and say

"I'm fine" but are hanging on by a thread to their life and salvation. After that sermon I felt to go to my friend and when I wrapped my arms around her, she wailed out and I wailed with her. I had no idea where that cry came from inside of me. I guess it was compassion.

She had been there for me at difficult times in my life and I could not believe that I couldn't help her. But God kept nudging me saying, "You're not God". I felt like a breakthrough had come that night but it didn't manifest itself for a few more months.

Then one Sunday she said, "*Pray for me, God is giving me favor. It looks like I am getting a house!*" It was everything my friend had prayed for in a home. Sometimes God takes his time. He knows when the time is right. Our will has to be broken so He can trust us with a blessing with no doubt that it is from Him.

When my friend told me of her answer to prayer, something leapt within me. I had been praying for healing and that was all the encouragement I needed to continue. I knew that God still answers prayer. He knows where we are, and what we need, and the perfect time to answer it.

I knew my miracle was coming.

IT TAKES FAITH TO RECEIVE

"Now unto him that is able to do exceeding abundantly above all that we ask or think, according to the power that worketh in us…"
Ephesians 3:20

Sometimes you can feel blind sided by a sickness or problem that attacks you until your faith is so low you see no end or help in sight. I had been struggling with a sickness so long it began to manifest itself in my spirit. I began to be broken by the infirmity and started feeling downcast and without hope – the opposite of what I usually am.

God let me come across a song by James Cleveland called *Where is your faith in God*, and the words struck a chord in me. It brought me to my senses. I began to ask myself where my faith in God was, that I could think that this is situation was permanent and had no room for change.

Through God, in an instant this sickness or problem could be taken care of. I put that song on repeat and listened to it until my thinking was renewed, and I began to remember the miracles God gave me in the past. Then, I really started believing for the one I needed now. A few days later God miraculously touched my body after I activated my faith and started believing again in God's healing, saving power. It truly does take faith to receive.

WHY CAN'T YOU BE HEALED?

"The Lord is good, a strong hold in the day of trouble; and He knoweth them that trust in him."
Nahum 1:7

Sometimes God speaks to us in the most unusual ways, and uses ordinary objects to help you understand. One night before church I was praying at the altar saying, "God, I need this healing", but I had been plagued by this condition two years and I was not seeing an end in sight. In fact I began to think this was the new me for the rest of my life.

But then, God talked to me in words I understood. We had an old Hammond organ in our church that I loved to play. It broke down and we were missing being able to play it and missing what it added to our services. We brought in expensive repairmen several times, and the next day it was broke again.

The music team were starting to say things like,

"Maybe there's no hope to fix it."
"Maybe it's done and not repairable."

But we didn't give up. We called in a repairman again even though it was expensive and tried one more time. And, yes, it was finally fixed and we were enjoying Hammond organ music once again.

As I was at the altar I looked up at that old organ which appeared beat up and old, but working like a charm and God spoke to my spirit, *"Well the organ is fixed, why can't you be healed?"* That sparked faith to continue to believe for my healing. God speaks to us in the most unusual ways.

YOU CAN TOUCH HIM

"Jesus said unto him, If thou canst believe, all things are possible to him that believeth."
Mark 9:23

You can touch Him
I can feel Him within my reach
You can touch Him
It is Jesus, you can touch Him
When you're in need, you can touch Him

Push past the doubt and unbelief that you can't reach Jesus. I often say, "Lord I believe, help my unbelief." We are human and sometimes the mountain in front of us seems impossible and discourages us. Our God understands we face times when it is hard to believe. He told Thomas come touch your finger to my side. Thomas couldn't believe it was really Jesus.

Whatever has you bound, you can touch Him,
He is just within your reach, you can touch Him.

I WILL ANSWER HIM

"He shall call upon me, and I will answer him:
I will be with him in trouble; I will deliver him…"
Psalms 91:15

Just ask the savior to help you. My father was a minister and at the end of his sermons, he would start out singing an altar call song.

Ask the Savior to help you
Comfort, strengthen and keep you
He is willing to aid you
He will carry you through

I'm so glad my dad taught me to call on God when I'm overwhelmed, sick, troubled, and most of all when I just don't know what to do. Just ask him to help you. It's an act of faith to ask the Lord to guide us.

When we doubt ourself or doubt Gods love for us we will not ask because we don't feel worthy. But try Him, and see what He will do.

"Looking unto Jesus the author and finisher of our faith; who for the joy that was set before him endured the cross, despising the shame, and is set down at the right hand of the throne of God."
Hebrews 12:2

DESPERATION WILL MOVE YOU

"And a certain woman, which had an issue of blood twelve years, and had suffered many things of many physicians, and had spent all that she had, and was still sick, but rather grew worse. When she had heard of Jesus, she pressed through the crowd and touched his garment. For she said, If I may touch but his clothes, I shall be whole."
Mark 5:25-28

A woman with an issue of blood suffered twelve years. She went from doctor to doctor with no answer. When you have suffered that long your faith becomes weak. You have prayed and prayed for an answer with no change.

Even though you know He can heal and that He shed blood for your healing, your mind can't comprehend why you haven't been healed. Keep believing, and ask friends to pray for you.

A trial can deplete your spirit. Maybe you have felt already that God has healed you because you had some good days, and thought the sickness was over… only for it to then return. Your faith can take a hit because you thought you were healed. Keep believing.

What you do when this happens is to keep declaring your healing by faith. When you get your healing the Lord can say like He did to the woman with an issue of blood, *"Thy faith hath made thee whole; go in peace, and be whole of thy plague."*

What will cause you to have great faith? Desperation will move you to great faith.

ASK AND YOU SHALL RECEIVE

"Ask, and it shall be given you; seek, and ye shall find; knock, and it shall be opened unto you: for every one that asketh receiveth; and he that seeketh findeth; and to him that knocketh it shall be opened."
Matthew 7:7-8

You can ask God, but the answer is like a package that you order – you're not sure when it is really coming. You are sure God heard your request, but not knowing when it is coming can be stressful.

Especially when you are sick and feel like you can't take many more days like this, God is still in control. He knows the process and what He is trying to accomplish through our trial. Just keep believing and worshiping.

There will be some days when you can't seem to touch God because your faith is low. Keep worshiping.

There will be days when God will break through and renew you in the spirit, in the midst of your trial. Oh what a refreshing. Even if you're not totally well, the presence of the Lord will be so powerful and renewing to your broken spirit. Your faith will be renewed to believe that package of healing is coming from above just like He promised you.

IN A MOMENT HE CAN TOUCH YOU

*"Bear ye one another's burdens,
and so fulfill the law of Christ."*
Galatians 6:2

When you are sick and in pain you can't imagine the end of the sickness. You are in it, it doesn't feel like you are coming out of it. The body is miserable when in pain. Sometimes you can't believe for yourself, so although you don't really want to tell others where you are, you have to reach out to others for prayer and let them have faith for you.

One bad day doesn't mean the next day has to be like that. In one moment God can change everything. So have a support group. People that will pray for you. When you feel like your back is against the wall and you see no way out, reach out to your prayer partners and let them intercede for you.

God designed it this way – that we could lean on each other and carry each other's burdens. When He brings you through it, you will be glad to be a testimony of his greatness.

TRUST GOD TO CARRY YOU THROUGH

When you suffer sickness, you see no way out. You have to lean on others' faith and your faith in God. Any small word of faith is like survival food for the soul.

You can't understand how God is getting any glory out of the pain you're in. You may feel like maybe you deserve it and maybe even that Jesus doesn't love you. That's a lie. While we suffer the same things the world suffers, we have a God we can call upon.

Sometimes I would lay in pain and keep saying, "*Jesus I know you love me.*" I remember how my dad would have our church recite that same phrase.

Keep saying it and after a few times and you start to believe it, even though the devil wants us to believe that God doesn't care about us. Sometimes you feel overwhelmed with pain and you begin to feel like it would be easier to die than live. Our times are in Gods hands. He doesn't bring things upon us, but allows us to endure it for a season. Situations can turn into our personal Job-like trial.

Job didn't understand what was going on in his trial. He was miserable. His wife and friends encouraged him to curse God and die. That would have been the easy way out. But Job said, "Though He slay me, yet will I trust Him". The devil was telling God that the only reason Job trusted Him is because He had been so good to Job. God blessed Job greater at the end of his life than at the first. But in the middle of his trial, he could not even imagine the blessings coming. Hang onto your faith in Him and trust in God to carry you through.

NOTHING MAKES YOU
MORE USABLE THAN PAIN

"And he went a little farther, and fell on his face, and prayed, saying, O my Father, if it be possible, let this cup pass from me: nevertheless not as I will, but as thou wilt."
Matthew 26:39

You are more like Jesus Christ when you suffer than at any other time. When you suffer, it feels like there is no end in sight. You can't imagine any good coming out of it. But one of the passages in the Bible that has always stood out to me is Ecclesiastes 7:3:

"Sorrow is better than laughter: for by the sadness of the countenance the heart is made better."

In sorrow we desire to hear God and what He is desiring from us. Laughter is just a good time with no learning.

WHERE THOSE HEALING WATERS FLOW

"And Jesus went about all the cities and villages, teaching in their synagogues, and preaching the gospel of the kingdom, and healing every sickness and every disease among the people."
Mathew 9:35

When you're in your trial, you feel there's no end in sight. No reprieve. No answer. But our God is our help and our reprieve.

"And the Lord, He it is that doth go before thee; He will be with thee, He will not fail thee, neither forsake thee: fear not, neither be dismayed."
Deuteronomy 31:8

Hold onto that lifeline with all that is within you and you will never be disappointed. God is our only hope. Doctors can disappoint because they do the best they can, but they did not make our bodies – God did.

Sometimes when we are sick and in pain, we feel like we are alone. But there are so many people suffering all over the world. Start praying for others while you are in pain.

COUNT YOUR BLESSINGS

"And, behold, I am with thee, and will keep thee in all places whither thou goest, and will bring thee again into this land; for I will not leave thee, until I have done that which I have spoken to thee of."
Genesis 28:15

What has God done for you today? Did He answer a prayer of yours? Maybe He didn't give you the whole answer, but maybe He gave you the desires of your heart for this day.

"This is the day which the Lord hath made; we will rejoice and be glad in it."
Psalms 118:24

Some days you're not totally well, but God knows. What you desire and want, He grants it according to His will. I was sick while we were on a family trip. I asked God that I would be able to attend church and even when I wasn't sure if I could make it, He gave me strength to be there. The preacher spoke right to me.

When God gives you a word when you need it, it is so sweet to the soul. I was able to enjoy Sunday dinner with family and visit for several hours. The whole day wasn't pain free, but God allowed me to enjoy the things that were important to me. I had to count my blessings in the midst of the pain.

It was almost as if He was there showing me that He was still there in my trial. He heard the desires of my heart. And though my full answer hadn't come yet, He was hearing me as I spoke to Him and He was answering me.

BE STILL AND KNOW

Be still, and know that I am God: I will be exalted among the heathen, I will be exalted in the earth.
Psalm 47:10

Have you ever told a child to be still as you're trying to put their shoes on? We can be like this too when God is doing a work in us and we won't stay still because we don't understand yet what's going on in our lives. We are striving to find a solution to our dilemma or situation on our own. We are so miserable we just keep trying to find our own way to fix it.

Finally we get still before the Lord and say, "I don't have the answer, I don't know what to do." It's then that you give our Heavenly Father a chance to step in and work on your behalf. As long as you're striving to fix it in your own strength, God has to step back until you turn it over to him saying, "Lord I don't know what to do, I need you. I trust you with this situation. You have never failed me. So here it is solve it as you choose."

It's a natural tendency as humans to want to fix our own problems. The more we learn to turn things over to God, the quicker the peace of God can calm us. If the problem or sickness isn't solved immediately God gives us peace so we can trust Him in the waiting process.

LAUGH LIKE SARAH

*Therefore Sarah laughed within herself,
saying, After I am waxed old shall I have
pleasure, my lord being old also?*
Genesis 18:12

Sometimes when you laugh like Sarah, it's because Gods plans for you are are so big and out of the norm, your mind cannot imagine how God is going to accomplish it. I have this famous saying if I can't imagine how something is going to be accomplished I just say *"Really?"* Sara was considering the state of her body and in her mind she was saying, *"Really?"*

God may promise you something but He doesn't always do it according to your thinking or your earthly timetable. He does it when all you can do is step back and laugh or say *"Wow, God. Really?"*

God wants to get all the glory for what He does. And He knows the appointed time of when things should happen.

WHEN I FALL I SHALL ARISE

"Rejoice not against me, O mine enemy: when I fall, I shall arise; when I sit in darkness, the Lord shall be a light unto me."
Micah 7:8

You can fall in many ways. You can fall from your desire to walk with God and from your desires for Godly things. You can fall in your health and sickness can bring you low, so low that you feel you can't do anything but be in pain, and can't even take care of yourself.

It's at these times when it's hard to keep speaking faith when you are depending on your loved ones to take care of you. Deep down you're a do-er and a worker and you look around and see so much that needs to be done, yet you have no strength to do it. So it sits in your eyesight undone. The ones that you would ask to take care of it are already taking care of you. You don't want to ask for one more thing.

But speak faith to yourself, even though it's hard. Utter praises to God. Rejoice as you trust and believe that your current trouble will not last, that God is your light and your salvation.

Jesus cares about you. The enemy may be whispering in your ear that "God has forgotten you" or, "You deserve this." But out-talk the enemy! Say "Jesus, I know you love me. I shall arise."

LORD YOU KNOW THE WAY I TAKE

"But he knoweth the way that I take: when he hath tried me, I shall come forth as gold."
Job 23:10

Sometimes the adversity or sickness you find yourself in leaves you with no answers or thought of where to go or what to do next. If you are confident in your love for God and his love for you, all you can do is praise Him with what strength you have and trust that God knows where you are. And when you come through this, the Word says you will come forth as gold

The trying of your faith is very painful and a place you wish you didn't have to be. But God knows where we're at. Tell Him, "I have nothing to go back to. The faith in You is all I have. I don't know where You're at, but You know where I am."

"P.S... Please Lord, come get me as soon as you can."

THE ANSWER IS ON ITS WAY

"And Jacob their father said unto them, Me have ye bereaved of my children: Joseph is not, and Simeon is not, and ye will take Benjamin away: all these things are against me."
Genesis 42:36

I was going through a time of constant sickness. It was like one thing ended and something else started. It kept me from enjoying and participating in things I usually took part in and took for granted.

I remember the moment when a despondent feeling came over me. Tears filled my eyes and I said, "Lord You've been so good to me. I know You're with me, but I need You to speak to me."

That is when the phrase "all these things are against me" came to my mind. So I looked it up in the Bible and found it in Genesis when Jacob's brothers came back from Egypt and told their father they had to take Benjamin back with them.

Jacob felt like he couldn't take one more hit or endure one more loss. He said "all these things are against me." But a few verses later we see that all his suffering was getting ready to have meaning. Joseph, the other son that he lost was for a purpose, and he was now able to preserve his entire family during the impending famine.

Just when Jacob felt like he couldn't take one more blow, the answer was on its way. He would discover he still had his son Joseph, and also the brothers that had been jealous and cruel to Joseph would now have the perfect opportunity to get their spirits right.

HE SETTETH ME UPON HIGH PLACES

"He maketh my feet like hinds' feet,
and setteth me upon my high places."
Psalms 18:33

I had been sick for weeks and I was beginning to feel it was impossible to feel good again. I knew God was able, but the sickness was trying to break my spirit of faith. I cried out, "Lord, I need a word from You. How is this all going to end, do You still have work for me in Your kingdom?"

And just as I thought that the scripture came to me, "He maketh my feet like hinds' feet, and setteth me upon my high places."

The word of God amazed me in that moment. I know His Word is true and that He is going to make my feet like hinds' feet even though I can barely walk in this moment, and He will set me in

high places. God is up to something great.
Believe for it!

WEEPING IS A PART OF LIFE

"For his anger endureth but a moment; in his favour is life: weeping may endure for a night, but joy cometh in the morning."
Psalms 30:5

You may have days where you're weeping and think something is wrong with you. Maybe you're weeping because you're in physical pain and you are grieving because you feel you are not able to do the things you normally do and you wonder, *"Will I always be like this?"* Maybe you grieve because of lost relationships that you can't seem to fix no matter what you try.

Weeping is a normal emotion in life, and God says weeping may endure for the night, but joy comes in the morning. Stand on that promise. Make a note write down everything that is making you weep. Maybe you're weeping over lost loved one that you have prayed over for so long. After you release in prayer the things that you're weeping about, start worshiping and praising God. Our God inhabits the praises of His people. Just weep, and then praise God. He will show up and turn your mourning into dancing. Make your tears count. Give them as an offering into the Lord.

"Thou hast turned for me my mourning into dancing..."
Psalms 30:11

A FOOTHOLD IN THE MIND

"Finally, brethren, whatsoever things are true, whatsoever things are honest, whatsoever things are just, whatsoever things are pure, whatsoever things are lovely, whatsoever things are of good report; if there be any virtue, and if there be any praise, think on these things."
Philippians 4:8

Sometimes Satan tries to get a foothold in the mind of a saint of God. He makes you fearful, dreading the days and not looking forward to anything. You know this is the enemy, because our heavenly father does not deal with His beloved children this way.

When this happens start a fast, and recite this scripture pushing the event back by worshiping and praising God. The closer we get to the end the enemy is working overtime on the committed children of God to give up in their mind. Hold on to the Lord!

IS MY ARM SHORT THAT I CANNOT SAVE

"Behold, the Lord's hand is not shortened,
that it cannot save; neither his ear heavy,
that it cannot hear…"
Isaiah 59:1

When you have an ongoing sickness that takes you away from your daily routines, it makes you second guess whether you can ever again do the things you have always done. You keep thinking real soon this whole thing will fly away and be gone… or that's what your daydream is.

Every time you go to a new doctor looking for answers you don't want to be there as the process goes on and on. You began to doubt yourself – maybe you don't deserve healing.

But then, you hear of others that have worse

situations than you do. You think that maybe you just need to settle that this is your lot in life.

Then you hear a voice speaking to your mind, "Is My arm short that I cannot save, is My ear dull that I cannot hear?" Something quickens in your spirit – the Lord is trying to reach you in your despair. A quickening of faith leaps from inside you.

In John Chapter 9, people were looking at a blind man and asking why this had happened to him, wondering among themselves that maybe his parents had sinned. But Jesus said, "So the works of God might be displayed in his life."

When your faith is weak, God brings back to mind things that will encourage you. I recall a song my father sung many times: *Have faith in God. Have faith in God. Have faith in God for deliverance, have faith in God.*

SHUT IN WITH GOD

When you're sick you are like the old song, *Shut in With God in a Secret Place*.

> *Shut in with God in a secret place*
> *There in the spirit, beholding His face*
> *Gaining new power to run in this race*
> *Oh, I love to be shut in with God*

We really don't ask to be shut in with God, but the severity of our situation causes us to get real close to God. He's our only answer; we don't know what to do. We know He's the only one we can turn to and be transparent with, and out of that deepest trial can be some of the greatest times in the spirit. As we seek his face everything pales in to comparison and we began to cherish the sweetness of our times in the presence of the Lord.

SEEK YE FIRST THE KINGDOM OF GOD

"Wherefore, if God so clothe the grass of the field, which to day is, and to morrow is cast into the oven, shall He not much more clothe you, O ye of little faith? Therefore take no thought, saying, What shall we eat? or, What shall we drink? or, Wherewithal shall we be clothed? (For after all these things do the Gentiles seek:) for your heavenly Father knoweth that ye have need of all these things. But seek ye first the kingdom of God, and his righteousness; and all these things shall be added unto you. Take therefore no thought for the morrow: for the morrow shall take thought for the things of itself. Sufficient unto the day is the evil thereof."

Matthew 6:30-34

I have found that if the enemy of your soul can get you to become worried about your future, your finances, and how you're going to live, you will become full of worry.

God wants us to be good stewards of what He gives us, but He doesn't want us to become dependent on our money and our provision. Instead, He wants us to look to Him as our everyday guide and provider.

Sometimes He may ask you to give an offering and you're thinking, *"God… I need this to live on."* Give it and watch Him give it back 100 fold. Give whatever God directs you to do. That's His will for you, and He will provide for you in the process.

Gods greatest desire for us is to be a channel of blessing. If He blesses us with abundance, it's to bless others and not think we have obtained it on our own. He trusts us to become a channel of blessing for others. You give, and it shall be given to you.

God does not give to us so we can look down on others saying, "Look what I have". But He can use your talents to bless you, so you can bless others. If we put him first, He will always be there for us.

"Give, and it shall be given unto you; good measure, pressed down, and shaken together, and running over, shall men give into your bosom. For with the same measure that ye mete withal it shall be measured to you again."
Luke 6:38

HOPE THOU IN GOD

You might find yourself sliding down the slippery slope of despair. You may truly be surprised when you find yourself at this point. I found myself there when I went through a siege of sickness. When one would let up, something else would show up. After several times of this happening, I began to doubt myself and lost confidence that I could handle what may be coming next.

My imagination was wondering what friends and family praying for me were beginning to think of me. Nobody likes to be in a helpless place. We like to be at the top of our game. Then we began to think maybe we brought this on ourselves.

I was in our Sunday service and I cried from my heart, "God, I feel hopeless today". A lady from our church walked up holding onto a devotional on hope. She said I've been enjoying this so much, but I felt to give it to you. While she was handing it to me she was reluctant to let it go. I knew for sure she was doing what God told her to do. God was talking to me in his loving way.

"I know you need hope – I know where you are at this time in your life."

How thankful I am for a loving God that cares where we are. Thank You, God, for Your love and kindness, for reaching me where I was that morning.

TRIED BY FIRE

"That the trial of your faith, being much more precious than of gold that perisheth, though it be tried with fire, might be found unto praise and honour and glory at the appearing of Jesus Christ"
I Peter 1:7

When you are tried by fire, you become very shaken. Everything you thought about God is set in concrete in your mind. Then comes this fierce trial that blows into your life. You still believe and determine that you won't give up your faith in God, but it's like you're blowing in the wind and you feel so shaken you become fearful. You cry out to God, "Help me!"

One day I felt like this when I Peter 1:13 came to me: *"Wherefore gird up the loins of your mind, be sober, and hope to the end for the grace that is to be brought unto you at the revelation of Jesus Christ."*

The most precious part of this scripture is my memories of my dad quoting this in Bible study to the saints. These memories gave me extra strength when I needed it most.

THE GREAT I AM PROVIDES FOR ME

"According as his divine power hath given unto us all things that pertain unto life and godliness, through the knowledge of him that hath called us to glory and virtue."
II Peter 1:3

I have lived a blessed life. I have things I don't deserve. I've been places, seen sights, and served in places that made me wonder, "How did this happen to me? I'm just a regular person."

All I can recall is God placed a love for Him in my heart to walk humbly before him, to do His will, be a blessing to His people. Encouraging, loving, helping. I'm not perfect by any means, yet I can testify that if you endeavor to put God first and be used by Him, that He really will use you for His glory.

There will be some very blessed times. There will be testing times. But when it's all done, you will be able to look at your life and say, "Only God." I'm living a blessed life.

VICTORY THROUGH THE SPIRIT

*"Then he answered and spake unto me, saying,
This is the word of the Lord unto Zerubbabel,
saying, Not by might, nor by power, but by my
spirit, saith the Lord of hosts."*
Zechariah 4:6

God wants to give you victory, but it won't be in your own power. You have to keep in touch with God daily and sometimes several times a day when you are in the hardest part of your sickness or inner pain.

*"Howbeit this kind goeth not out
but by prayer and fasting."*
Mathew 17:21

Fasting is a powerful tool. It's not easy to do, but both God and the enemy know you are serious. When you fast, let your request be made known.

Get a trusted friend praying with you when you feel like you need it. The enemy doesn't like it when you turn to God in earnest. As long as the enemy can make you feel you are backed in a corner with no way out, He's got you whipped and beat down.

But when you fast, pray and reach out for prayer – He doesn't like that kind of defense. He's no match for that. We are no match for our trials, we have to claim and win victory through the spirit.

I STILL BELIEVE

"Then saith he to Thomas, reach hither thy finger, and behold my hands; and reach hither thy hand, and thrust it into my side: and be not faithless, but believing."
John 20:27

Sometimes life's ups and downs toss you for a while, and everything you believe gets tested and tried. You're weary in mind and you begin to doubt yourself. You may start to think God wants you to live like this, maybe this is His will for you to be sick, or to carry this burden.

Then a God-thought breaks through and a measure of faith strikes like a fire shut up in your bones. Then you remember the Bible says, "By His stripes I am healed."

"But He was wounded for our transgressions,
He was bruised for our iniquities: the
chastisement of our peace was upon him;
and with his stripes we are healed."
Isaiah 53:5

I am set free. He died that I might be saved, healed, and delivered. I still believe He is able to do it for me, because it's not His will that any should perish.

"The Lord is not slack concerning his promise, as
some men count slackness; but is longsuffering
to us-ward, not willing that any should perish, but
that all should come to repentance."
II Peter 3:9

In my desperation, I'll believe that deliverance is for me and I'll let my faith reach up and touch the throne of God. I will start singing with excitement: *"I still believe, I still believe."*

MY GRACE IS SUFFICIENT

"And He said unto me, My grace is sufficient for thee: for my strength is made perfect in weakness. Most gladly therefore will I rather glory in my infirmities, that the power of Christ may rest upon me."
II Corinthians 12:9

Whatever you're going through, God's Grace is sufficient. We like to feel strong and healthy and wise, but when we don't have the answers to life's problems we are more dependent on God, and our weakness is something God can work through.

When I am weak, I am strong in the Lord. His Word tells us that a meek and a contrite spirit is one He can use. We think exactly opposite. We think if we are strong, then we can do something for Him... but He doesn't want our strength. He wants to be mirrored through us.

Many will be drawn to God through our weakness to give them hope that there is an answer for their needs. If God can help you , give you favor and strength, then He could do that for them.

NOTHING SATISFIES

"Trust in him at all times; ye people,
pour out your heart before him:
God is a refuge for us. Selah."
Psalms 62:8

"O God, thou art my God; early will I seek thee:
my soul thirsteth for thee, my flesh longeth for
thee in a dry and thirsty land, where no water is."
Psalms 63:1

There's nothing like the feeling of pouring your heart out to God as you earnestly seek Him. I found myself in a foreign land after several days of traveling, doing good things for the Lord, but not finding that time I needed with God.

My heart got so heavy that nothing satisfied, and I felt physically sick in my spirit. I laid on my bed that night and said, "God I have no prayer closet to go to but I will pray silently in my mind."

Earnestly I sought him. "God if you don't touch me with a fresh touch of Your spirit, nothing else will satisfy. Seeing and preaching around the world is a privilege, but it does not satisfy if I don't have that close communion with you."

If you don't have that special time with God, the enemy can start piling on all kinds of negative feelings and emotions. He will try to bring up problems from the past, and overwhelm you with the tasks set before you. But one sweet time in God's presence is all you need where you cry out, "I need you Lord. Nothing in life is worth it or enjoyable if You don't touch me once again with Your spirit."

Oh the joys of our relationship with our Savior. Nothing is enjoyable if your spirit is not in tune with His. The best place to be is where our hearts find themselves in one accord with God's. Nothing between us. No hurt, no trouble, no sorrow that we have not fully shared with him.

That's the way our Heavenly Father desires it.

ONE MORE STEP

"When I remember thee upon my bed, and meditate on thee in the night watches. Because thou hast been my help, therefore in the shadow of thy wings will I rejoice."
Psalms 63:6-7

Our Savior is ever present. He is so near to us, even on our bed before sleep. Our spirit may not feel all is well, and we can cry out to Him. Remind Him again He has promised to heal your body, and heal your spirit. Whatever your need is remind Him of His promises.

It's desperation that brings on great faith. "God, I can't go one more step – something has to change. When I wake in the morning, I want to be a new person in Christ Jesus. It will happen."

GOD'S SCHOOL OF FAITH

"But without faith it is impossible to please him: for he that cometh to God must believe that He is, and that He is a rewarder of them that diligently seek him."
Hebrews 11:6

Hebrews 11:6 tells us that without faith it is impossible to please God. But how do we acquire faith? Certainly, it is developed through trials and sufferings that we would prefer not to go through. These test our hearts, our strength, and can develop faith in God. If there were no trials in life, you would not need or know about having faith in God.

When you suffer, you are most like Jesus Christ. He suffered for our salvation and He took stripes for our healing. Like Jesus cried out on the cross, "If it be so let this cup pass from me," we also at times in our suffering cry out in anguish, "Please let this suffering pass from me".

We never know what is happening in our life when we are suffering, but we can trust the God that died for us that He has us in the palm of His hand. He said He would never leave us nor forsake us.

"There shall not any man be able to stand before thee all the days of thy life: as I was with Moses, so I will be with thee: I will not fail thee, nor forsake thee."
Joshua 1:5.

So whatever trial or suffering you find yourself in today, remember that God is with you. He is not punishing you. He is making something beautiful out of your trial. You will be able to look back with faith and see His hand in yours the whole way. You're in God's School of Faith.

HE MAKES A WAY WHERE THERE IS NO WAY

I woke up in a foreign country with a headache that was very debilitating. My doctor back home advised me to find a chiropractor while I'm traveling in case this were to happen. He even sent me with a letter telling them what they need to do in order to adjust me properly.

I woke up that morning and I was in dire need. My husband had already called one time to the nearby chiropractor and asked for an appointment, but he said he couldn't because he was too busy.

The next day I was in such pain my husband waited outside the Chiropractor's office and was going to ask him again in person. A man arrived and my husband said, "Are you the Chiropractor?" He said, "No, I do acupuncture." However as he told him my problem, he said,

"Acupuncture would be good for her; bring her to my office."

With a morning full of visits, he worked me in. God gave us favor with him. He wasn't going to charge us, but we insisted. It helped me I was now well enough to handle two days of air travel to get home.

Sometimes in the midst of your worst times God will break through with a silver lining to help you and encourage you. I still marvel today that God gave that man a desire to help a complete stranger that he may never see again. Only God can make a way where there seems to be no way.

THIS IS THE WILL OF GOD FOR YOU

"In every thing give thanks: for this is the will of God in Christ Jesus concerning you."
1 Thessalonians 5:18 KJV

I had been in bed suffering with an illness where I had been progressively losing my quality of life. Slowly but surely, the ability to experience good things I was use to were slipping away from me. The medication that was suppose to help me was not helping me for the better. I had friends, family, and my church family praying for me. There were times I thought I was healed and had even told my doctor I was, and then the illness came roaring back with its symptoms.

My husband and I do overseas ministry, and at one point I felt like I was in a good place. I scheduled a 30 day trip with him, yet only made it 14 days before the illness manifested itself and I came home early by myself and let my husband fulfill our obligations. I came home fighting not only this sickness, but jet lag and the feeling of defeat. This brought on some very low days, but I made it through with close family and friends helping and praying for me. I had more doctors appointments set up, at a very well-known place. However, I wasn't really looking forward to it. By this time I had went from doctor to doctor with no long lasting change. I really was out of my comfort zone going to doctors. I just wasn't excited.

I did travel to these new appointments and I had another MRI. When I was in the MRI I prayed, "Lord let Your light from heaven shine on me in this MRI and show them what needs to be done." When I went to the doctor for results he said, "I know what problem you have and I can

do a procedure tomorrow to take care of it."
That was so fast… tomorrow!

I had to get away by myself and ask the Lord if
this was my answer – is this what I need to do.
As I sat in a hotel lobby, which was my makeshift prayer room, a scripture came to my mind:
*"This is the will of God in Christ Jesus concerning
you."* I Thessalonians 5:8 was impressed upon
my spirit that this was my answer, to face the
procedure with confidence from God.

Keep the word of God in your mind daily. Even
though I didn't know where that scripture was in
the Bible. I had known it since Bible study nights
as a child. God spoke His word and I had
confidence to face the procedure, knowing it
was right for me.

I WILL EXTOL THEE

"I will extol thee, O Lord; for thou hast lifted me up, and hast not made my foes to rejoice over me. O Lord my God, I cried unto thee, and thou hast healed me."
Psalms 30:1-2

When the Lord comes through with the miracle you've been praying for, it's like you just can't quit praising Him. You are so thankful as you remember how the trial was so hard and long and painful. When He sets you free, you can't praise Him enough. You can't worship Him enough. The great God of the universe heard your cry and delivered you. There are not enough words to thank Him for what He's done. Your Heavenly Father heard your prayer and He has answered it.

HE GOES BEFORE ME

*"He giveth power to the faint; and to them that
have no might he increaseth strength."*
Isaiah 40:29

This problem had been going on for two years,
and those that loved me and cared for me didn't
know what to do. Days before my miracle, I was
asking daily God give me a word for each day, a
song to sing. I would sing to cast out fear and
anxiety, as the pain that was trying to overtake
me and said, *"there is no hope."*

I frequently ask the Lord to give me a song. I
love music, and frequently sing songs over and
over in my mind or play them on my phone.
Songs are like my constant companion. God
never disappoints – I usually get my word or
song first thing in the morning.

As always, our God is close to the broken hearted. He gives comfort to those who trust in Him.

There is a song called Psalms 23 (I am not alone). Verse one says,

"The Lord is my Shepherd
He goes before me
Defender behind me
I won't fear"

I couldn't remember the rest of the lyric, but those lines were my life line before, and during, my deliverance. In fact, it still is my theme song afterwards. As I faced a procedure God was bringing to light answers for my problem, but I still needed to make tough decisions. That's a hard place to be, constantly wondering *"God, is this right for me? Is this the way for me?"* It's a very scary place if you don't have God giving you a word, and my word was this song.

What is there to fear? He's going before me, and coming behind me. I'm covered! But in our mind, we fight feelings of being unworthy. We tend to question what is so special about us that He would care so much?

God told me the answer: You are my child. If you're a normal parent, there is nothing that you wouldn't do to protect, comfort and help your child through the situations of life. Our God's love is so much greater than human love. I find myself so thankful as I walk this road called life – I am not alone.

THE SONG OF DELIVERANCE

"Now faith is the substance of things hoped for, the evidence of things not seen."
Hebrews 11:1

The best way to obtain a miracle is get a song of praise and worship and keep it in your mind and on your lips even before your miracle.

My husband preaches that the children at the Red Sea were weeping and crying for fear before the Red Sea parted. Pharaoh's army was behind them, the seemingly uncrossable Red Sea before them. After God parted the waters, they had no problem praising and thanking God… but they should have done that before their miracle.

When I look at my own life, I notice that the songs that I am singing after my miracle are the songs God gave me before it happened. God gave me these songs because I asked. I was so low in spirit waiting for deliverance I was asking daily. God give me a word, give me a song. Then I would sing all day long. I knew God was my only hope, and that my answer would come through Him.

A couple weeks before my deliverance, I asked God to give me a song and the next morning as soon as my eyes opened, and before my feet touched the floor, the song came:

"You made a way
When our backs were against the wall
And it looked as if it was over
You, You made a way
And we're standing here
Only because You made a way"

Written by Travis Greene

When I was singing that song, I was truly singing it by faith. I could see no way out, no answer in sight, and yet I chose to truly worship and praise God, trusting that He would see me through to deliverance.

Worship really is the way that the battle is won. What came to my mind after deliverance was that the same songs that brought my miracle were the ones I am singing after my miracle. Praise and worship is truly the way to your miracle, leaning totally on God.

THE LIE OF SHAME

Something can happen when you have been sick for a long time, and you have been praying, but the answer is delayed: the enemy makes sure that you feel shame. When you have been that person that is looked to for answers and has prayed for others, lifting them up during their times of trial, then you go through a time of extended sickness and become the one that needs help and prayers, you no longer are the one that others come to for answers and prayers.

This trial of your soul will go on until you feel you have no more strength to endure. It's crushing. I don't know anyone that would *want* to endure something like that. However, if you have wanted to be close to the Lord and do His will, and if you become what He needs you to become, you become willing to go through a crushing to get out all of yourself, so He can fill you back up with His likeness.

In that process you may end up in a place where you are so low that you may feel shame. All you thought you were, all your pride, all your ego, all of what you thought you brought to the world is now emptied out.

Our Heavenly Father endured this also. After going about healing others, as He was facing Calvary, the ultimate sacrifice, He was so weak He couldn't carry his own cross up the Golgotha hill. He was taunted, "If you are who you say you are, come down off the cross. Save yourself!" He cried out to let the cup pass from Him.

However, Jesus had to endure the pain and shame because He wanted to pay the price for humanity's sin. Our Savior was tempted in all points like we were, yet without sin. We have to endure the shame to be partners with Him to accomplish our purpose in this world.

EPILOUGE

As you read this book about my suffering and pain, you will probably wonder what it was that I was going through. My problem was Trigeminal Neuralgia; a nerve disorder in my left eye that took two years to diagnose. I went through several MRIs, saw many different doctors, and endured many days of suffering without knowing what was really causing my problem.

God finally led me to the right hospital and doctor– Mayo Clinic was an answer for me. They diagnosed me one day, and did Gamma Knife Radiosurgery the next day. This answer and procedure was a blessing , but the emotions I went through with such a fast answer to my prayer was an experience in itself. We are so used to praying for answers, but when they come, sometimes we question and hesitate to proceed. My husband preaches a message about how Jesus bears long with you and suddenly the answer will come (Luke 18:7-8). I got alone with God which was the only spot I could go to– the hotel lobby turned into my makeshift prayer room as I talked to God in my mind, which was all I could do at the moment.

I told God about others that I know who had this problem have had other surgeries, but they are offering me this alternative non-invasive procedure and how I was wondering if was right for me. "Is this my answer?" God spoke to my mind these words from 1 Thessalonians 5:18: "… for this is the will of God in Christ Jesus concerning you."

God amazed me at that moment. I knew immediately this was my answer, and went forward in faith. I had prayed for two years for healing. God impressed me, "Don't look at what my answer was for others. This is the way of escape I provided for you."

The procedure was painless and immediately fixed my problem. I went home the same day in awe and rejoicing that God really does hear and answer prayer. A physician had previously started me on medicine for the problem, and two weeks after this procedure, I was able to stop. While I could have stopped it that day as I knew my trial was over, in respect to the doctors I followed their plan.

To this day I still have the reminder on my phone, it pops up every morning – "Take your medicine". I take this time every day to stop and thank God for hearing and answering prayer. I hope you found something in this book that will cause you to have a deeper faith and trust in God.

Victory to Victory

TRIUMPH THROUGH PAIN

Also available on Amazon.com

The Battle is the Lord's: *Devotions for Tough Times*

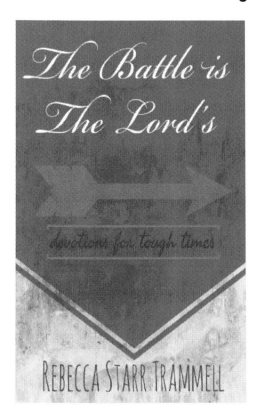

Made in the USA
Columbia, SC
26 February 2024

32035679R10072